Discover
Your
Dragon

Emre,
Get
over
here !

by

Kungfu-Cious

MoCap

Mortal
Kombat

Discover
Your
Dragon

5 Steps 功夫

to the 健 行

Victorious Life 平 衡

技 術

目 標

by

Kungfu-Cious

Donald Hyun Kiolbassa

Discover Your Dragon
5 Steps to the Victorious Life

© 2012 Donald Hyun Kiolbassa
and KungFu-Cious Media
www.kungfu-cious.com
All Rights Reserved. Published 2012.
Printed in the United States of America
21 20 19 18 17 16 15 14   3 4 5

ISBN: 978-0-9836035-1-1

Published by First Flight Books
A division of Bruce Bendinger Creative Communications, Inc.
2144 N. Hudson • Chicago, IL 60614
773-871-1179 • www.firstflightbooks.com

Editor: Bruce Bendinger
Production Editor: Patrick Aylward
Cover Design: Andy Wong
Cover Photo: Erika Dufour • www.erikadufour.com

*To my father and mother
for making me the man that I am today.*

Contents

Hard Work

Health

Balance

Skills

Goals

Kung Fu Consciousness
PREFACE

Hello. I am your guide, **Kung Fu-Cious**. This is short for "Kung Fu Consciousness" – a way of thinking to achieve results in life.

I had the honor of winning a gold medal at the 2008 World Games as Captain of the United States Chinese Martial Arts team.

I have had the honor of being one of the few foreigners in the world allowed to live and train in seclusion at the legendary Shaolin Temple.

During my time there, I learned much about martial arts, but more importantly I learned a lot about life.

This book is my gift to you – the first steps on the path to "The Victorious Life." I learned how an Eastern approach can bring success in modern Western Society.

The first step is simple.

Turn the page.

In general, Kung Fu refers to what you accomplish through hard work.

"The Victorious Life" offers you a greater chance of success – but, like all things, it comes at a price.

This book will show you the first five steps on this path. Taking these five steps will also help you "Discover Your Dragon."

In Western culture, the Dragon is often viewed as a villain. Bedtime stories often end with the "Hero" slaying the Dragon.

However, in Eastern culture the Dragon is viewed much differently.

The Dragon is a symbol of success, representing balance, strength and honor – sacred in the Chinese Culture, acting as guardian of the balance between the human world and the spirit world.

In this book, we will help you take the first steps to discover the Dragon inside of you.

You will find these first steps surprisingly useful in a wide range of activities. In fact, they can change your life. They changed mine.

As a half European/half Asian kid growing up in Chicago, I was never quite "American" enough nor "Asian" enough to fit in any specific group.

In some ways I was an outcast. Martial arts created a path for me to protect myself and to establish my identity. Then it showed me more – a road to excellence and success far more important than fighting off bullies.

I wrote this book to share that path with you.

My own background is in the martial arts. Here, life is serious business.

While the losers no longer die – unless, of course, it is in a video game or an action movie – still, the game of life deserves our best.

In life, victors achieve more than a high score.

We no longer slice through bodily organs with a razor-sharp samurai sword – but we still work to cut through obstacles.

As we move together through the five powerful principles in this book, you may discover how to conquer the habits that can become our own worst enemies.

Taking these steps will help you teach yourself how to excel, succeed, and win.

Many of these things are worth saying more than once. In the East, things are repeated until they are remembered without effort.

This book will offer you five small steps which contain five large lessons – five big things, which you can use to form a solid base of success in your own life.

But first, I think I will tell you a story…

My Journey to the Shaolin Temple
INTRODUCTION

When I was 27, I lived with the legendary Shaolin Monks at the Shaolin Temple. It was a time spent in seclusion where I could truly focus without distraction.

The Shaolin Temple is a Buddhist monastery located in China. It is famously known as the birthplace of all contemporary martial arts. Though I did not know it at the time, it would change my life.

Stories of the Shaolin Temple meet somewhere at the intersection of reality and legend – all are anchored by a strong history of tradition.

Tales of the Shaolin Temple have been exaggerated, twisted, and manipulated for storytelling purposes. Sometimes one comes to believe that the Monks are more sorcerers than warriors, since the tales of their abilities seem almost magical.

The Shaolin Temple provides a breathtaking

landscape for martial arts training. The ancient temples are tucked within a forest and guarded by mountains.

Originally, I thought I was going there so I could train to fight, but, as I soon found out, this place would teach me much more.

I would, as the book's title indicates, "discover my dragon." And take those first important steps on the road to "The Victorious Life."

I was far from home in a strange, unfriendly world. I thought to myself, "You are in over your head. You do not belong here."

The Shaolin Temple Training Chamber –
Tools of the Temple

Living as a Monk is extremely difficult. The living quarters do not provide the things we are used to – like hot water for showers. The daily training regimen is brutal. It begins with a 4:30 AM wake up call. That's right, 4:30 AM.

From then on, my face constantly seemed covered in a mixture of sweat and dirt from training in the mountains with the Monks.

The day begins with a warm up consisting of a several mile run from the sleeping quarters to one of the many surrounding mountains.

The mountain range looked like an insurmountable adversary. Conquering even one mountain seemed impossible for someone like me.

A frigid October breeze engulfed the mountain range. It sent chills up my spine.

It made my heart shiver. My knees jittered as I started up the cold merciless mountains.

I was literally a stranger in a strange land, with no one to help me. Alone. On my own.

This was a particularly cold morning. I vividly remember filling up two buckets with water. Once the buckets were filled I was instructed to climb the mountain without spilling any of the water.

I was told that this was an ancient traditional form of martial arts training, and it was critical that I should be careful, and I should not spill any water out of my buckets.

Ancient tradition? I saw ancient craziness. What does carrying buckets of water have to do with learning how to fight?

At the time, I did not realize the impact these two buckets would have on my life.

I do remember picking them up for the first time. The frigid air made the tin handles painful to hold. I joked about the shape of the buckets. They had a cone shape on the bottom.

The Monks laughed. One of them turned to me and explained that we were not allowed to use buckets with flat bottoms, because flat bottoms would give us the chance to set the buckets down to rest.

These buckets had cone shaped bottoms, so if you ever tried to rest the bucket on the ground, the water would spill out. Then, you would have to start over.

As I lifted the buckets, I felt an intense strain in my shoulders. That was just the beginning.

Walking up the mountain was, in itself, a treacherous challenge. The base of the mountain had trails, which zigzagged up. This made the walk extremely slow and unpredictable.

The trail was about three feet wide, flanked on each side by thick and rugged shrubs. The shrubs provided their own discipline – with ample thorns to accompany my journey.

As I made my way through these unfriendly shrubs, I was occasionally startled by wildlife springing out onto the trail.

After we had climbed hundreds of feet up the side of the mountain, the nature of the path changed. Now, a worn concrete staircase greeted us. I felt a sense of terror.

My body ignored the frigid breeze, which sliced through my silk training outfit like an icy knife.

We were now in single-file, moving upwards at a fast pace. Step by step we climbed up that worn and narrow corridor of stairs.

Cold as it was, sweat was streaming down my face. I felt a growing pain in my shoulders and legs.

The steps were so steep and narrow that looking down it seemed almost like a vertical drop. The higher we went, the more surreal it became. The landscape was amazing. The mountains were eye-level and draped in a soft blanket of clouds.

But I was in no mood to enjoy the scenery.

It was during this moment that I was reminded of my extreme fear of heights. My body collapsed into a kneeling position. But I did not spill the water.

Kneeling there, I completely stopped the rest of the procession behind me.

I was both humiliated and frightened, locked in a battle with my own feelings of loneliness, pain, and exhaustion.

After a few moments, the Monk behind me spoke quietly. He simply advised me that there was a long line behind me, and the stairs were so narrow that I could not turn around.

Sometimes, even in the middle of difficulty, things are simple. The only way to go was up.

His calm words echoed in my mind, "Do not look down." I slowly stood up and continued my climb one foot at a time. I heard frustrated yells coming from behind me, I shut them out and focused. Slowly I took one step at a time.

I barely made it to the top of the mountain without spilling the water. I was dizzy from the altitude and exhausted from the climb.

My lungs were burning from the thinness of the air, and my shoulders felt as though they had been pulled from their sockets. My hands and my entire consciousness were occupied with the buckets. My own sweat became a painful enemy, stinging as it dripped into my eyes. I was unable to even wipe my forehead.

We continued to carry the buckets of water until we reached the top. Then each of us was placed in front of a tree. My arms were screaming for a rest. My breath was as labored as I can ever remember.

It took all my efforts to keep from vomiting after that incredible climb. What happened next shook me to the foundations of my logic and reasoning.

Monks began to water the plants around the tree that stood before them. I was not only exhausted, but I was utterly confused and angry.

Why the heck did we climb that mountain?

I risked injury and death, and I could barely lift my arms.

My mood shifted. With cold anger, I asked: "What does watering plants have to do with martial arts training?"

The Shaolin Temple Mountain Range

The answer I was given changed my entire perspective on life.

I was told that here, in the Temple, martial arts is not about teaching ways to kill.

It is about teaching ways to live.

At that moment, my journey truly began…

Hard Work

功夫

Climbing Mountains is Hard Work!

We are each at the bottom of our own mountain.

Now we will climb together.

To succeed through Kung Fu Consciousness we must first understand and accept that climbing the mountains of life is hard work.

To begin, you must believe in yourself. I know that this can be easier said than done. How do we build up the strength to climb our mountains?

The first step is to master Kung Fu!

We must learn to work hard.

These are two of the most misused Chinese words in Western civilization – Kung Fu. I cannot help but chuckle every time I hear these important words misused.

Kung Fu does not translate to "martial arts." It actually means "Hard Work."

Despite the incorrect translation, the term is still very important. Hard work is of immense importance for success in your field.

What is your field? It does not matter.

You may think you already work hard. You do not. Your first step is to truly learn to work your hardest.

The practice of Kung Fu is a self-discovery process that builds your capability, your strengths, and your self-confidence.

When you truly embrace Kung Fu, you will learn to push yourself to your limits. You will begin to discover what you are really made of and you will grow stronger.

This means that you need to take your training very seriously. Things will not just happen in life. You must go out and make them happen – and sometimes it can be a difficult climb.

There are four elements to Kung Fu, which will guide our journey. They are: Discipline, Accountability, Tenacity, and Confidence.

ᗷloody Knuckles
DISCIPLINE

Discipline is the cornerstone of hard work.

Without discipline, your hard work lacks the consistency it needs to grow and develop.

I really learned the concept of discipline while living at the Shaolin Temple.

During one particularly brutal training session, the head martial Monk instructed us to start practicing basic punches and kicks on wooden dummies and punching bags.

After a few hours, I noticed that this was the only exercise being practiced.

My knuckles became bloody and dirty. Sweat streamed down my forehead. What was the point of this exercise?

Blood was now pouring from my knuckles as my skin was being ripped off. I could feel my skin dangling from my knuckles, as I kept punching at the lifeless wooden dummy.

Enough! I'd had it! I became frustrated because I found the repetition unproductive as well as bloody and painful. I sought counsel from the Monk instructor and demanded a higher level of practice.

The Monk guided me to The Shaolin Temple Pagoda Garden. We walked through the garden as he explained the importance of pagodas.

In the Shaolin Temple Pagoda Garden

Pagodas are dome structures with a spire at the top rising vertically towards the sky.

Legend says that pagodas act as a lighthouse to the spirit world. Every time lightning strikes the pagoda, it is a spirit traveling to Earth.

As we toured the Shaolin Pagoda Garden, I had the unique opportunity to witness some of the structures. The concrete spires were rooted in the soil and soared to the skies. The delicate craftsmanship caught my eye. The aged beige of the pagoda contrasted with the fresh green of the garden.

However, I felt as if the Monk was avoiding the subject. I asked him again the reasoning behind what seemed to me redundant basic training.

He exhaled an extended breath of frustration and asked me, "Do you remember when you learned to breathe? Or rather do you think about the correct way to breathe? A person breathes so much everyday that they do not think about it, they just do it."

This simple answer brought clarity.

I saw the purpose in what seemed to me meaningless repetition.

Think about it.

Most activities in life are done through pure instinct. We have learned via repetition. We breathe. We drink. We sleep. Our instincts are our basic training. They are literally that – "instinctive."

Through repetition, we move from conscious to the unconscious – Kung-Fu-Consciousness.

This principle is one of the most influential concepts in your personal development – we must learn past conscious learning. Throughout life there will be times when we will need to depend on those "basics." What's more, we must do them without thinking about them.

How do we get there? Hard work.

You drill your basics through repetition, and your instincts flow from those basics. There will come critical times in your life when you will need to rely on your basics and instincts – because things will be moving too quickly for you to plan appropriately.

The first step to building your own personal discipline will be your ability to keep working hard and consistently to achieve your goals. You must have the discipline of consistent repetition. And you must outwork the competition.

Your competition is out there, working hard. A few bloody knuckles will not stop them.

Keep at it. The harder you push, the better you will become.

Discipline can be difficult for many people.

I mean, think about it. Discipline is no fun.

It is painful. It is time-consuming. Generally, you do not see immediate results. You get no glory – just sore shoulders and bloody knuckles. But the repetition of practice is critical for you to develop.

It is easy to fall into a comfort zone and never go past that boring point where you begin to build the discipline you need. Remember – discipline builds your foundation, and that helps you grow.

In whatever you do, try to work past your comfort zone. Try to find a way to sustain your focus past "the boredom barrier."

Try this. Work to keep yourself interested in your practice by always exposing yourself to new challenges. When you start feeling too comfortable and you do not have new challenges to face, practice becomes mind numbing. At those moments, it's easy to lose interest and question whether the cost is worth the reward.

It is. Those who "Discover Their Dragon" know how to pay the price. It begins with discipline.

A simple first step to implement discipline in your life is scheduling. Something as basic as showing up on time demonstrates discipline – to yourself and others.

We all have things we have to do – add a bit of discipline to those daily activities.

Prepare a schedule in advance. Write it down.

To the world, it is simply your daily "To Do" list. But, to you, it is your *Daily Discipline Workout*.

Prioritize and get things done!

Skip the late show if it conflicts with an objective on your checklist.

This sacrifice is an investment in your future.

Even in everyday activities, you can find opportunities to improve. Make improvement a habit.

Find new challenges to push yourself and your practice to new levels. You will achieve new levels of skill and new levels of discipline.

When your practice brings you to a place of mastery, reinvent yourself. Become a student of something else.

You will find that the habits of discipline will make each mountain easier to climb. You will put your feet more firmly on the path.

Making Your Bed
ACCOUNTABILITY

You must hold yourself accountable. This is the next major element of Kung Fu.

What good is a schedule if you don't enforce it? Discipline is meaningless without enforcement.

Accountability helps you evaluate yourself.

I call this, the "Look in the Mirror" exercise.

Can you honestly look yourself in the mirror, and say that you are sticking to your discipline and growing?

There were times in my life when I could not. It happens to all of us.

This is a story of one of those instances.

The Shaolin Temple is virtually a self-sufficient city. The Temple supports and funds various civil functions – including an orphanage. This orphanage accepts children from all over the region.

The orphanage provides food, shelter, education – and martial arts training.

In fact, on a side note, many of the orphans who display a strong martial ability are later re-cruited by the Shaolin Temple to become Monks.

Each day an orphan is charged with a specific task. On one occasion the trainees were partnered with the orphans to assist in the day's task. My partner was a little girl, approximately 12 years old. We were charged with making the beds of the orphanage.

At first, I did an extremely poor job of making the beds. Frankly, I took a somewhat lax attitude towards the job. I noticed that every bed that I worked on was not properly made.

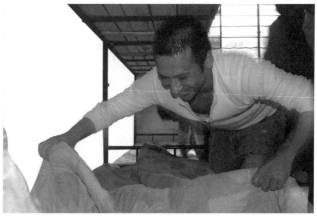

Making Beds at the Shaolin Temple Orphanage

The little girl would redo the beds until they were perfect. Unfortunately, she did not have time to remake every bed after my inadequate attempts.

Upon inspection, the head martial Monk came in and was very displeased. I was not too worried. I figured his arms must have grown somewhat fatigued from beating me so much.

The head Monk questioned the poor quality of some of the work, and, before I could assume responsibility, the little girl jumped up and told him that she was in charge of oversight, so she took full responsibility of the mistake.

I was floored!!! And I was ashamed. She was taken out of the room and punished severely. Poor quality work is not something they tolerate at the Temple. Her blood was on my hands.

When she returned, I asked why she took the blame when it was clearly my fault. The tears swelled in her eyes as her choked voice squeaked out, "Your actions and my actions become our actions." I was speechless and embarrassed.

I was speechless at the depth of this simple

response and embarrassed that my poor actions hurt someone else. It was not a proud moment for me. Her voice echoed in my ears and replayed over and over in my head.

It was my turn to cry. Tears streamed from my eyes. It is one thing when our actions humiliate our own honor, but it is completely different when our actions hurt someone else.

I could not look at myself in the mirror.

When you work with a group, you represent that group. When one party acts, that action is a reflection of the entire group. I was part of her group, and my poor action reflected on her.

Make Your Bed properly! At the end of the day, you will have to sleep in the bed you make.

The next day I was extremely diligent in making the beds. We never had the issue again.

If I had held myself accountable, all of this could have been avoided. Like so many things in life, it is difficult but simple. But we can learn.

Hold yourself accountable to your practice. You must be able to take an honest look at yourself, and stick to your discipline.

If you are not holding yourself accountable, you are cheating yourself and all those around you.

The job itself does not matter. Sweeping floors. Carrying water. Making beds. Our world is full of small tasks that must be done. It is accountability that matters.

When we do a careless job on menial tasks, we demean ourselves. When we hold ourselves accountable, someone is always watching.

Do not settle for average. See if your work product is superior. If it is not, work to improve. Accountability is a long-term process.

At the Shaolin Temple Orphanage with My Teammate

Try not to be too negative or positive during your self-evaluation. You need a balance of negative feedback and positive reinforcement.

If improvement does not come, consider a change. You may need a change to reach your maximum output ability. If you decide to make a change, make it quickly.

A simple way to practice accountability is to enforce the schedule you made earlier.

When you put something on your schedule, do not go to sleep unless it is finished or, if necessary, rescheduled. Do not allow ordinary tasks to be rescheduled more than three (3) times, unless there are extraordinary circumstances.

This process can be painful. Frankly, sometimes it will suck. Life always seems to find a way to get in the path of your plans. The key to success is to consistently find ways to get things done even when life gets in the way.

Another quick tip – surround yourself with those who are trying to accomplish their own tasks.

As much as possible, be with people who hold themselves accountable. This will push you to perform better. It will improve the quality of both your life and your friendships.

If people seem to be constantly rescheduling or talking about what they wish to do – without ever really doing these things – then you may wish to remove them from your equation.

Or, if they are people who are important to you, help them if you can.

Remember, at the end of the day, you sleep in the bed you make, and your daily actions affect others around you.

Take a deep breath. Commit to these small, but important aspects of your behavior. Hard Work. Accountability. Discipline.

Now that you have begun to develop discipline with *Bloody Knuckles* and you have decided to hold yourself accountable by *Making Your Bed*, it is time to work on the next important element – *Tenacity.*

Never give up – even when you occasionally fail.

Foot Binding
TENACITY

Here is something to think about.

Our current successes are based on previous failures. Before we learned to walk, we fell on our little baby butt. Life is like that.

We will fail a lot in life. We all do. Get over it. The key is to not focus on our defeats, shortcomings, or failures. They can be steps to success.

At some point, you will be knocked down. It is not a question of *if*, but *when* you will fall. The real question is how quickly will you get up and recover.

Now you understand why a key building block of Kung Fu is tenacity – the ability to consistently endure failure or hardship and keep moving forward.

Failure gives us perspective on the degree of difficulty we face in achieving victory. It also helps us develop respect. Respect for yourself and respect for the task at hand.

Respect for yourself is important, because it forces you to perform at your highest level. It is when you are performing at your highest level that you will truly discover yourself.

Most of us don't begin as winners.

When I first started in martial arts, I always seemed to be the underdog. I am not physically intimidating and on top of that, in a male dominated practice, my martial arts instructor was a woman.

Training

My coach was a professional Chinese martial artist. She had her own issues – she always seemed to have a tough time gaining respect.

Martial arts is a sport where it is assumed that the most physically dominating figures are the most powerful. Looks can be deceiving.

Sometimes the most power comes from the smallest packages.

Historically, women in China did not hold much social, political, or financial power. They were expected to be delicate flowers. One measure of their delicateness was the size of their feet.

For hundreds of years, China had a practice called "Foot Binding" for women. Parents would tightly bind their daughter's feet with bandages to keep the size of the feet small.

The bandages were so tightly wound they would restrict the growth of the girl's foot by literally breaking it. It was extremely painful to say the least.

Binding would keep the girl's foot small and force her to walk in a very delicate manner. It was simultaneously a sign of both elegance and obedience to a man.

It was a painfully oppressive process that generations of Chinese women were forced to endure.

I could not imagine walking with two broken feet for the rest of my life!

It makes my stomach turn to think about it.

Today, Chinese women, and women in general, have had to fight many battles to overcome their obstacles.

Their strength is more apparent then ever.

I saw that strength evidenced in my teacher's fierce tenacity to keep fighting despite hardships.

She had to face many challenges in proving her ability in our sport.

I was as guilty as the next man. When I first saw her, I questioned her ability. I thought, how could a woman compete against the men? The male competitors looked so much more dominating.

All doubt was erased seeing her in action. She would lure her male competitors into a false sense of security, as she stalked her prey like a black widow. Just when you would let your guard down and question her ability, she would pounce before you could react. I fell victim to this myself on more occasions than I would like to admit.

The first lesson she taught me was never underestimate anyone. Never. Anyone.

My coach struggled to gain respect from her male counterparts, and she was constantly put in a position to prove her ability. She didn't win every time. Nobody does.

People knocked her over and kicked her while she was down because of who she was in this sport. But no matter how many times she was pushed down, she would get up and push back.

People tried to "Bind Her Feet," but she always fought back and broke free of those restrictions.

She was judged because of her gender. It fueled her motivation. When she was perceived as weak, she pushed to demonstrate strength.

Her drive inspired me to fight – no matter how people perceived me.

She was always on a mission.

Her mission became my mission.

In whatever you do, do not expect a smooth path upwards. To get there, you may have to walk with broken feet.

People will knock you over and kick you when you are down. You must have the tenacity to get back up and fight. Fight like your life depends on it, because, in many ways, it does.

Toughen up!

Do not allow society to bind your feet.

Set achievable goals and then work to achieve them. Step by step.

Students need to toughen up. We learn that failure is part of the game. Teachers need to follow up a student's failures with both negative feedback and positive reinforcement.

The problem arises when failure is combined with negative reinforcement and no progress. This can be especially difficult for young children, teenagers, and adults with poor self-confidence. Unbind your feet.

Make mistakes. But learn from them.

A simple way to practice tenacity is to stick to that schedule you made.

You made a schedule to build your *discipline*. Now you are enforcing your schedule through *accountability.* Keep at it. Keep at it even when you are knocked down. Keep at it even if your initial plans do not work out.

There will be many obstacles in your life that will knock you down. Your ability to get back up will determine how far you get.

If you are tenacious, you will be successful, because if you keep trying you will eventually succeed.

Discipline. Accountability. Tenacity.

They are hard work.

But they will help you grow and they will help you build self-confidence.

Breaking Bricks
CONFIDENCE

Your hard work – your Kung Fu – will develop your self-confidence. The elements of discipline, accountability, and tenacity will begin to support the weight of your growing confidence.

It's an important ingredient to your success. Confidence leads to risk taking – sensible risk taking – and risk taking leads you to try new things.

After all, if you do not try, how can you succeed? If you always do the same old thing, how can you grow?

Something that always amazed me at the Shaolin Temple was the practice of "Hard Body Qigong."

Qigong (Pronounced CHEE-GONG) is the practice of energy manipulation to harden your body. When the Monks would harden their bodies, they could smash bricks with theirs heads or absorb devastating hits to their neck or crotch.

It looked almost superhuman. My jaw dropped as I witnessed an 80-year-old Monk stab a spear into his neck. The spear broke and he walked away unharmed. When we would get together after training, we would challenge him to break metal chopsticks using his throat.

I was only asked to break a brick with my hands. The first time I tried to break the brick, I was so intimidated that the brick won before we even started. I struck down at the brick, but the brick was not phased. I screamed. My hand felt broken.

The brick didn't care, and it was not phased by my chop. My confidence sank. Once again, I was consumed by shame and humiliation.

That night I battled insomnia as the day's epic public failure replayed in my mind. I had my swollen hand on ice, and my battered ego resting.

As I looked up at my ceiling trying to ignore the footsteps of the scurrying mice, I heard one of the Monks outside my door – he was one of the Monks assigned to train me.

He was checking up on us before bed. Despite

his broken English, he always had a scholarly way of expressing himself in one-sentence life lessons.

He said simply, "No bird flies on its first try, but it still must believe it can fly or it will fall." These words echoed in my mind, and I fell into a deep meditation thinking about it.

One cool thing about living at a Buddhist Martial Arts Temple in China is that all the Monks seem to have profound quotes for every situation.

You are going to fail in the beginning, but if you do not believe you can succeed, then you have already lost.

Training on Pillars in the Shaolin Temple Garden

Think about it: when you do not believe in yourself, you can feel it. You perform poorly or not at all, and you generally do not push for your best.

With these thoughts, I immediately fell asleep. In the morning, I was prepared to break my brick. But I would go step by step.

I needed to build my confidence, so I took a step back. I also needed to heal my injured hand.

I began by breaking wooden boards. I gradually moved to larger and thicker boards. By the time my hand recovered and my technique improved, I was confident in my ability.

I was ready to face my nemesis. By the time I got to the brick, my confidence allowed my energy to flow freely. The energy hardened my body – I broke the brick in one strike. My eyes widened and my confidence grew as I smashed through that brick.

Just as I smashed the brick, I turned to my left and watched a little kid break the same kind of brick with his head. I chuckled at my small victory.

Build your confidence in steps. Set small goals

– ones that you can manage. I like the way that martial arts grows a person's self-confidence. The reasoning is that in every stage of martial arts training you try and fail until you succeed.

So, for example, if you are trying to learn something new in school or at work, do not expect to "get" it on your first try. One technique is to break it up into smaller subsections.

Focus solely on a particular subsection and build from there. Step by Step.

Try not to bite off more than you can chew.

The only time we are guaranteed to fail is when we do not try.

People with self-confidence can go almost anywhere and do almost anything.

They succeed because they are willing to try. They understand that they may need to try over and over again, but at some point they will succeed.

Many people focus on some of my accomplishments without paying attention to the fairly long laundry list of failures I accumulated in life.

Try new things. Do not be afraid to fail.

Step outside of your comfort zone. Stay interested in your practice by always exposing yourself to new challenges.

Understand that steps to success may include a stumble or two – or an unbroken brick and an almost broken hand.

Strive for new challenges.

Focus on achievable goals. Make them goals that you actually want to achieve. For example, I think I'll take a pass on that thing where you break metal chopsticks on your neck.

Steps You Can Take

As you journey up your mountain, you will come across a few bricks you will need to break. You cannot break the bricks of life without getting a few bloody knuckles.

To do this takes hard work. You will need *discipline*, *accountability*, and *tenacity*.

Throughout this chapter we discussed some small, but practical ways to develop those habits of hard work – your Kung Fu.

Create a daily checklist (*Discipline*). Enforce that checklist (*Accountability*). Keep at it even when times get tough (*Tenacity*). As you grow, step outside your comfort zone and try new things (*Self-Confidence*).

There are many ways to implement Kung Fu in your life, but a very important factor is to find your own source of *Motivation*.

You need to be working toward something, which motivates you to go through all these struggles. There must be some reason that pushes you to endure the struggle to succeed.

What motivates you? Find it. This motivation will fuel your desire to succeed. This desire will make you want to improve your Kung Fu.

And working harder will be easier for you.

An easy way to make Kung Fu part of your life is the checklist system. It is simple, but difficult.

Create your daily checklist of things you need to accomplish. Do not try to list too many things to do. And understand the value of repetition – accomplish the same thing, day after day.

Carry your checklist in your pocket.

Make a new one everyday.

Your checklist should include time to study and practice. Every day you will take steps towards building yourself into your desired end product.

Skip that extra round of video games and get your chores done. It is also alright to miss your favorite television show to make sure you get all your work done.

No matter how busy your life gets, never

forget your daily list. Have the discipline to make it before you begin your day. Some people do it in the morning – others the night before. Just do it.

Be accountable!

Be tenacious! Failure is practicing to succeed. Stick to your checklist – even when things do not work out, or when progress seems slow.

This part is bloody difficult. Nobody likes to fail. Worse, discipline and tenacity can be boring. It can be a painful process. But it is good for you.

The good news: you will be improving as a person. Think of it this way: If it was easy, then anyone could do it, and your accomplishments would not carry any value.

Stick to your discipline and accountability even when you are knocked down. Be tenacious. If you keep at it, you will be climbing the mountain.

Finally, force yourself out of your comfort zone. Try new things. Every week you should try something that is out of your comfort zone.

You will discover a world full of new adventures.

Whether it is as complicated and challenging as going back to school or as simple as trying a new food, go out and see a different point of view. Then, expand yours.

Expose yourself to outside influences. Life can get pretty boring and repetitive when you go through the motions of the day without challenging yourself. When you challenge yourself, you will grow as a person.

It is the mountain that each of us climbs.

Health

Prepare For Your Climb

In the previous chapter, we learned that mountain climbing is hard work. We need to be physically and mentally prepared to climb that mountain.

Your next step in achieving Kung Fu Consciousness is keeping yourself healthy.

YOU are your greatest resource in life. At the Shaolin Temple I learned a lot about the Eastern interpretation of healthy living.

For example, I remember when I was first introduced to Tai Chi. It looked like an interesting group activity, but I always sort of chuckled when people told me it was a martial art. I thought to myself, "What practical purpose would be served by moving super slow in a fight?"

Once again, I learned that sometimes the most important things come to you in ways you least expect.

First, I learned that "Tai Chi" is actually pronounced "Taijiquan" (Pronounced "TAI-Gee-shuawn"). But for simplicity, we can stick with "Tai Chi."

I also learned that Tai Chi is literally translated to "Supreme Martial Art."

The reason for this bold proclamation is due to the specific focus of this art.

It is focused on your health, and the originators of the art take the position that health is the *supreme* concern in fighting.

Think about it: if you are not healthy you cannot perform at your best. The movements of Tai Chi mimic fighting applied in a very slow manner, while massaging specific internal organs similar to yoga – but in a combat context.

Massaging the internal organs squeezes out the toxins, which build up in all of us. With the correct movements, the toxins are forced out of your body. How about that?

Ironically, you are using fighting applications to promote life and health. Once again, martial arts teaches us ways to live.

First and foremost, you need your health to operate at your maximum potential.

This is easier said than done.

We are a society hooked on caffeine, sugar, and fast food. We see the results from our waistlines to our high levels of blood pressure.

Perhaps we cannot help all of society, but we can help ourselves to better health.

An unhealthy lifestyle is not completely our fault. Society in general, and the food industry in particular, pushes many unhealthy practices down our throats.

Sad to say, unhealthy living is big business.

Our favorite athletes promote energy drinks loaded in sugar and caffeine.

Fast food companies have huge marketing budgets to sell you their processed foods with dangerous levels of sodium and fat.

Every one of them works hard to take your money and keep you addicted to their products. Sophisticated businessmen and research teams work to get you hooked – and keep you hooked.

They even try hooking you before you are capable of thinking for yourself. Big businesses aggressively market sugar-loaded products to us as children with cartoons and jingles.

If they get you early enough it can create an almost irreversible lifestyle.

But with discipline, accountability and tenacity, you can battle these clever enemies. They are the enemies of your health and the enemies of your wallet.

It must be your choice to live a healthy lifestyle. That choice will determine the type of life you will live. It will not always be an easy choice. The healthy lifestyle does not have a convenient Drive-Thru Window.

Though, occasionally, there is a Dollar Menu.

Living healthy will not guarantee you will be healthy. Sometimes things come up, which are out of our control, but living healthy gives us our best shot.

Your health, your vitality, is the engine that you need to help you achieve your goals in other aspects of your life.

Honor the precious gift you have been given. Make your health a priority.

To simplify things, let's focus on two critical aspects of your overall health – physical health and mental health.

The Vehicle For Your Soul
PHYSICAL HEALTH

Just like a car is a vehicle for you, your body is the vehicle for your soul – and that vehicle and the warranty that comes with it have limits.

Both a car and a body have limited life spans, and the length of that life span depends on the way you operate and maintain your vehicle.

If you crash your car or fail to maintain it properly, the quality and length of your journey will be affected – it's as simple as that.

But there's a major difference between the car and the body – you can buy a new car.

That body of yours will be the only one you have as long as you live. Take care of it as if your life depends on it. Because it does.

In many ways, your physical health is directly related to your output in life.

There are two major ways to maintain your physical health – exercise and diet.

Exercise:
The Origin of Martial Arts

The Shaolin Temple is historically known as the birthplace of martial arts. Many have heard of the Monks' mysterious practices.

Authors spin tales of the Temple like a comic book. These tales depict the constant struggle of good against evil.

These entertaining stories distract us from the practical questions. What are Shaolin Martial Arts? Why the heck are they practiced by Monks?

It does seem somewhat counter-intuitive that Monks, known for peace, would practice this.

When the first Monks began to practice, they would focus on meditation to experience peace.

Unfortunately, they discovered that if you sit around and meditate all day, your body slowly breaks down. Just like a car, you have to take it out for a spin once in a while.

For proper maintenance of their original equipment, they began to practice martial arts. You can't just sit around thinking of doing things.

You have to do them.

Healthy exercise is critical to your life. If the body is the vehicle of your soul, then exercise is part of the maintenance you need to ensure proper operation.

When the Monks took me into the mountains, we would do all sorts of combat training. But there was one form of combat that I always found kind of weird.

Front Jump Kick with Rope Dagger

The Shaolin Monks developed a particular style of martial arts that would mimic different wild animals.

I'd heard about "Animal Style" Kung Fu from cartoons and movies, but for me there seemed to be little practical value.

I'm a simple guy. I did not see much value in a fight by acting like an animal.

The first time I was trained this way, I felt really silly. I was on a mountain, pretending to move like an animal. Carrying buckets of water was painful, but I understood it. Skipping around like an animal seemed silly at best and humiliating at worst.

During a break, I asked the reasoning behind acting like a tiger or a monkey. The trainer smiled, and we discussed the wildlife in the forest.

The Shaolin Temple is located in a mountain range surrounded by forests. The Monks studied the wild animals around them, and learned how the animals defended and attacked.

They studied animals such as the tiger, crane, mantis, snake, and monkey.

The Monks believe that animals are the true warriors of the Earth. Think about it. In the wild, animals are constantly faced with life or death every second of their existence. The only rule in the wild is survival of the fittest or the fastest. In many ways life is the same way.

Animals are this planet's original warriors. So the Monks created their combat system based on these original warriors.

For example, the tiger style of martial arts is powerful and explosive. The tiger stalks in stealth, waiting for the right opportunity to pounce. This is an ideal exercise for a muscular, explosive person.

On the other hand, the snake is more elusive and sneaky. The snake hides in plain sight. This is an ideal approach for a leaner, quicker person.

I am not suggesting that everyone go out and learn tiger or snake style martial arts, but I do know that there is an exercise style for each of us.

Finding that style is part of your journey. To begin, put down the video game controller, the channel changer, and the comic books.

We are animals – not vegetables.

Now is the time to become more active in your daily life. Regular physical activities must be part of your path to better health.

What activity is best for you?

For a start, pick one you enjoy. Whether it is martial arts or soccer, basketball with others or a good run alone. Sports and other physical activities

Praying Mantis Training at the Shaolin Temple Park

are critical to maintaining your health. They exercise the muscles and stimulate the organs.

Try a Tai Chi class – surely there is one near you. Search it out.

Without healthy exercise, your body will be out of balance. Treat yourself right – your body is a truly marvelous machine – it deserves your best attention.

Today, many traditional Shaolin martial arts styles have been replaced by a more scientific approach to martial arts and combat.

And, of course, other forms of exercise are beneficial. I enjoy gymnastics.

So I probably won't go out and start fighting like a tiger anytime soon, but there is still much to learn from these original styles of exercise, derived from our planet's first warriors: the animals.

The key is to find the exercise that is right for you – the one that helps balance your life – and then keep doing it for all of what I hope will be a very long life.

Next step. Once we start moving our bodies, we need to give them the proper fuel.

Diet:
Chopsticks

Going to climb a mountain? Bring your chopsticks.

You're going to get hungry along the way.

Diet is the other important factor in dealing with your health. You are what you eat, literally.

On a rudimentary level, your body is comprised of cells. Those cells are produced from the things we put in our bodies – the things we eat and drink.

So, does it make sense for you to put things in your body that cause damage? Of course not. Certainly we can celebrate once in a while, but that should be the exception and not the rule.

When we cook something, the end product is the sum of the ingredients. If you use spoiled ingredients, your end product will be spoiled as well.

The Shaolin Monks have a very interesting approach to diet. They follow a strict vegetarian lifestyle while training. This is partially based on religious beliefs, but the main reason is health.

My teachers believed that the Earth is the "Mother" to humans, and gives us the gift of life by providing the necessary resources to live – like food.

The Earth gives us this as a gift to share energy, and we give that energy back as we live and die – sort of nature's recycling program.

Dining with the Shaolin Monks was a truly amazing experience. The Monks eat in a dimly lit mess hall that resembles a cafeteria.

At this point, you do not speak. While you are in the dining hall, speaking is strictly forbidden. Violating this rule leads to severe punishment.

The bowl and chop sticks set in front of you.

Well, you might wonder, how do you get your food if you cannot speak? When you sit, you get a bowl with a pair of chopsticks in front of you.

The chopsticks indicate where the food goes and how much you want.

Then, a few Monks begin walking around the tables with huge pots of food. To ask for food, you simply tap your chopsticks at the point in the bowl where you want the food.

The placement of the chopsticks determines the amount of food you are given.

The food is mostly rice and steamed vegetables, but the Monks also derive necessary protein from large amounts of tofu. Another rule – you cannot leave until you finish every last bite in your bowl.

The Monks take this rule very seriously. They do not believe in wasting food.

At first, the plant-based diet was difficult. I was raised on the typical American fast food diet – high sugar, high sodium, high carbohydrate, and high fat. That diet has only one thing going for it – it's cheap and easy.

When I was forced to live on the Shaolin's vegetarian diet, my body experienced intense detoxification.

It was like I was an addict flushing the toxins

out of my system. At first, it was extremely painful. I felt tired and weak.

My body rejected many of the foods, and without getting into detail, I lost quite a bit of weight.

Then, my body began to adjust. I started to notice significant positive differences. I no longer relied on meat, caffeine, or sugar to function. I had more natural energy – I'd broken the hold those hidden enemies had on my health and eating habits.

I'm not suggesting that everyone go out and become a vegetarian eating tofu instead of meat, but perhaps it is time for you to think about your own cuisine renaissance.

Consider trying different diet programs. There is no magic diet, and different programs work differently for different people. But you should start to think about what you eat. You can do better than burgers and fries.

It can be a difficult process, even more so here in the outside world than in the Shaolin Temple, where there is little choice.

In the United States, we have almost too much choice. But it is a conscious step that we all need to take – each of us finding a healthier way to eat.

After all, your life depends on it.

Take baby steps.

Start by taking control of your diet.

Regulate what you put in your body. Think about it. Buy a cookbook that appeals to you. Shop at different stores. Try new things. Become your own food inspector.

Cooking can be fun. You learn and develop new skills and it gives you a sense of ownership in your creations. Most importantly, you begin to really pay attention to what you put in your body.

There are many diets out there. Find the one that works for you. Your body will tell you.

We have become a society of consumers. Here in this fast food nation, we like our food cheap, big, and fast. I understand that companies need to make money, but at what cost?

If it is at the cost of our health, perhaps that is too high a price to pay for a Dollar Menu.

You can do this. You already have discipline, accountability, and tenacity.

Now you can practice Kung Fu three more times a day – breakfast, lunch, and dinner, and, perhaps, a light snack if it is too long between meals.

At the end of the day your body will become what you give it.

Respect yourself and that marvelous machine you were born with. Take the time to put in the correct fuel. This is one more important step in your journey to make yourself the best.

Exercise and diet are two aspects of maintaining optimal physical health.

There is another kind of health that is also important.

the Itchy Nose
MENTAL HEALTH

To climb our mountain we must be mentally focused, otherwise we may lose our way.

Your mental health is just as important as your physical health. You must have mental clarity and focus to be mentally healthy. If you have too many issues flying through your brain, you will be inefficient and become mentally exhausted.

You will not perform at your most effective level – stress will develop.

I wish we were taught mental health and clarity when we were young. Lack of focus hurts our output, and the lack of organization leads to stress and wasted effort.

Then again, most adults are even more stressed. How can they teach what they do not know?

Stress seems to accumulate as we become adults. It should be no surprise that mental stress can also affect you physically.

For example, if you are stressed, you might not sleep properly. Sleep deprivation will affect your energy.

One Eastern practice that can improve your mental health is meditation. At the Shaolin Temple, they take meditation very seriously.

In fact, if you talk or move during meditation, one of the Monks will strike you.

They use a paddle with studs. Ouch.

In the beginning, meditation was an extremely frustrating exercise for me. I struggled to understand it. My biggest problem? I was restless.

Generally, we would practice in the warm comfort of the heated meditation chamber – with a slight dash of incense in the air to create a relaxing aura in the room.

However, on one occasion the Monk in charge of meditation felt that the relaxed atmosphere made it too easy for us to meditate.

So he made us meditate at an extremely high altitude in the mountains. The winds felt like they would blow us off of the edge.

The dizzying height gave us a feeling full of stress and more than a little altitude sickness.

The meditation Monk instructed us to blank out our minds and focus on our breathing.

As I shut my eyes I found some humor in the irony that the Monks always seemed to have me practice at extremely high altitudes when they know I have a fear of heights.

Apprehensively, I blanked out my mind.

I only thought about my breathing. My mind went dark. This lasted about 15 seconds.

The winds made my nose itch.

After about 30 seconds, I could not meditate. All I could think about was my itching nose.

My entire train of thought was captured by the urge to scratch my nose.

It would be such a blissful feeling to scratch that itch. I couldn't take it anymore. I scratched my nose to relieve the irritation of the itch.

Within seconds, a flurry of blows rained upon my body – on my back and the tender sides of my stomach. The head Monk unleashed blow after blow upon me with his trusty wooden paddle.

That night, I tried to explain to my instructor that my nose had been itching. He responded, "So what?"

He further stated, "Your desire to scratch your itch distracted you from your breathing."

I started to understand his point.

In life, things will always get in the way. We will always have an urge to scratch some itch. Something somewhere will distract us. Always.

But if you scratch every time you itch, you will lose your focus and your ability to concentrate on the task at hand.

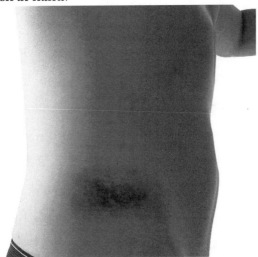

A souvenir – wounds from the Meditation Chamber

We must look past these distractions and focus on our goal.

In this case, just breathing.

I was ready to meditate the next day. I blanked out my mind and focused on my breathing.

Sure enough, the itch returned to challenge me.

This time I ignored the itch. I simply focused more on my breathing. The only thing I felt was my lungs expanding and contracting.

I slowly began to turn my attention to my heartbeat. When I felt in complete control, I turned my focus to the rest of my body.

I'd made a breakthrough.

My body felt like a well-rehearsed orchestra. The human body is truly a marvel of nature – a composite of some of the most complex instruments in the universe working together.

More importantly, that itch and the desire to scratch it were gone.

When distractions surface, do not let these small enemies defeat you. They are a tiny army waiting to keep you from your goal.

Focus on your goal even more. The distraction will often go away on its own.

Meditation teaches you to stay focused. We will not defeat every tiny enemy. But we will do better if we do not surrender to every little itch.

At this point, I really began to understand the practice. My mind understood it. My body understood it.

In fact, I still use this practice today – though at a lower attitude.

We have become too stressed in our lives!

The demands of school, work, and society are always there to shake our focus. For a few moments every day, we need to simplify our lives, find what is really important to us, and "just breathe."

Mental health begins with you. A great start is to create a moment of inner calm and focus.

You can do this. Just breathe. For just a moment you can conquer the distractions of life.

As you meditate, you will find it easier to put things in perspective.

You're alive, that's what's important.

Honor your life. Every day, give yourself the gift of calm and a clear mind. Just breathe.

Meditate. Focus on your breathing.

Then, expand to other issues. This will help improve your focus and your ability to accomplish your goals.

Life will have ups and downs. There will be many events that cause stress and be outside of your control.

For a moment, think only of your breathing. Just breathe.

Steps You Can Take

Health is of *supreme* importance as you climb the mountain of life.

Good physical health requires both healthy exercise and a diet that's right for you. We need to take our vehicle out for a spin once in a while.

Wherever we travel on the journey of life we should fuel up and eat properly.

Finally, we need mental health.

Developing focus through meditation is a good first step. We must win the battle over life's small distractions. Easy to say. Hard to do.

There are many ways to approach better health, but here is an approach to consider.

Set health goals for yourself.

Some people may have a specific health issue, like losing weight or getting in better shape. Others may just need to maintain themselves. Try to create goals with manageable and measurable results in your training.

Find the combination that works for you.

Set up an exercise program. We may not need to learn Tiger Style Kung Fu, but we can all use a little physical activity at least three times a week. Take that Tai Chi class. Meet with friends for a weekly basketball game.

Make sure you squeeze in that workout even when you are exhausted from school or work.

Be disciplined, accountable, and tenacious. Pick an activity. Create a schedule and stick to it.

Establish a healthy diet in your lifestyle. You do not have to become a vegetarian or adhere to some crazy diet, but you will still have to fight all those small enemies of the fast food army that lie in wait to make you gain weight.

Put down that extra slice of pizza. Add a salad. Avoid the calorie- and caffeine-packed latté. Try some tea instead.

This is tough stuff. Diets can be extremely complex, particularly since everyone has different nutritional needs. Try to find the best fit for you.

Even when things get tough, you must stay tenacious enough to get this job done. Win the battle against distraction.

Finally, give your mental health appropriate attention. Try to meditate.

I've found Yoga instructors to be excellent teachers of meditation, and they are very accessible.

Yoga is an easy way to learn meditation, because the instructors will have the practice in place for you. However, if this is not possible, a simple tip would be to meditate yourself to sleep every night.

Or, if you are an early riser, find a meditation moment in the morning.

Don't let small issues stress you out.

Defeat the army of small enemies.

Victory can have a big impact on your life.

Balance

平衡

Discover Your Dragon

You must be physically and mentally prepared to climb your mountain.

But to do well, you need more.

Your next step is developing balance.

You must have balance to travel a path that may be full of twists, turns, and unexpected surprises.

Just like babies must learn to balance as they take their first steps in life, you must work to stay steady as you take your journey.

The key to walking is balance. Seems simple right? Without balance you will fall.

The further you go on your journey, the more important this becomes. Yet, it's something we often take for granted.

When we achieve balance, we live the life of a Dragon. This might sound kind of strange, but hear me out.

Life is not only training and working out.

To the Monks, education is equally important. They know that in addition to exercising your body, you must exercise your mind.

The Monks offer many classes besides martial arts. These classes include language, literature, history, and so on. Often times, I found myself in the classroom "hitting the books."

My favorite subject was Chinese literature.

I learned much about life from these stories.

My teacher used to tell me that in every quart of fiction is a cup of fact. I smiled at the joke.

It was funny, but it was also true.

Some authors use stories to share lessons of life. My favorite storybook creature is the Chinese Dragon – a sacred creature in Chinese culture.

It is a great honor to be compared to the Dragon. It implies strength, power, and honor. It also demands *balance*.

In Chinese mythology, the Dragon is the guardian of the spirit world.

Dragons come to the rescue, breathing fire in the face of evil. To do their job, they split time between the spirit world and the human world.

The Dragon stands for moral good.

When either humans or spirits step out of line, the Dragon flies in and delivers Dragon justice, crushing the guilty party with its mighty claws and fire-breathing jaws.

The Dragons balance the needs and desires of both the human and spirit world.

Balance. Achieving it is not an easy task.

Often, the two worlds would be in conflict. The Dragon would then need to accommodate multiple interests to achieve peace.

Although the Dragon may not live in our reality, it symbolizes the importance of balance in our lives. We all have to fight our way through multiple and conflicting interests.

Everyone, from the teenager studying in school to the parent raising a family, must balance multiple interests and responsibilities in life.

In this chapter we will search for our balance point in a complicated world. From that point, we can accomplish much. This is the key thought as you work to "Discover Your Dragon."

What is balance?

Why is balance so important?

Finally, how do we balance our own life as we climb our mountain?

Let's start walking...

Yin and Yang
WHAT IS BALANCE?

Let's define balance as it applies to our own lives. This may seem difficult since each of us has a different balance point.

How do you define something that varies from person to person?

Let's use a symbol to explain the concept. Yin and Yang – one of the most influential symbols in Asian Culture.

The simple mainstream definition of Yin and Yang is the balance of two opposing forces.

However, this definition is incomplete. Life does not often work in complete opposites. There are many points in between.

Let's look more closely at the Yin and Yang symbol.

It is not just opposites.

Look more closely. You see that in every Yin there is a Yang and vice versa.

The "Yin and Yang" shows us that "balance" is the *management of multiple coexisting interests.*

We do not live in a world of clear-cut categories. Life is not always "black and white." There will always be "in betweens" in your life to complicate matters. More small enemies.

Just as the Dragon is required to manage the interests of both the spirit world and the human world, you, too, must manage your different worlds.

School. Job. Family. Friendships. And relationships that are more-than-friendship. It's complicated.

That's why you have to keep your balance.

Juggling these interests and responsibilities can be overwhelming for even the most balanced people. We deal with such issues as health, family, education, and career. Decisions in each of these categories can have huge impacts on your life.

At times these interests will be conflicting; at times they will compliment each other.

In each case, you need to find a balance point

for your interests in life. A simple mathematical approach might be to rank them in order of importance, and giving the most important its respective share of your energy and time.

Ah, if only it were that simple.

It isn't. But it is. Settle in.

In a basic way, you know what balance is. Try to stay centered on what you believe to be your best balance point. Try to feel it.

Do we know all the answers? Do we know what the future will bring? Of course not. But can we stay balanced as we move through the future? Yes. One step at a time.

Now let's talk about why balance is so important.

the Samurai Sword
THE IMPORTANCE
OF BALANCE

We just discussed The Eastern idea of balance – Yin and Yang, with a bit of Yin in the Yang and a bit of Yang in the Yin. It keeps things in balance.

Our ability to walk up our mountain also relies on our sense of balance.

We take alternate steps – left and right. We walk forward. And sometimes we must fight our way through obstacles.

Let's look at it through the eyes of a weapon.

The Katana was the weapon of choice for the Japanese Samurai. A clean and polished Katana creates a mirror-like reflection in the blade. Not only can you see yourself in the sword, but it also becomes an extension of your body.

Where is this going? What is the relationship between this sword and balance?

Let's take a closer look.

The Katana

In practice, your strong hand is placed near the top of the handle. The strong hand is responsible for "pushing" the curved blade.

Your weaker hand is placed near the bottom of the handle. This hand is for "pulling" the blade.

The Katana is an elegant tool capable of brutal, yet controlled destruction.

Its power comes from balance. The Samurai's push and pull technique is a balanced attack.

Two opposite forces work together to harness maximum power.

Balance is important. It creates *maximum output*. Balance requires managing multiple forces. If you manage them properly, you create synergy.

Push

Pull

This amplifies power.

The Dragon combines the energy of the spirit world with the energy of the human world.

The Dragon manages coexisting interests. *Discover Your Dragon* and you can do the same.

You can balance your circumstances to create maximum output in your life.

Complicated? Maybe. But it's also simple.

Think about walking. You instinctively balance as you coordinate your right leg with your left leg to walk properly. Together you move forward.

Obviously, life gets much more complicated than alternating your right leg and your left leg. Instinctively, we know that one leg won't do it. Inside each of us, we understand balance.

Take that first step. Then shift your weight and follow it with the next step.

Recall my experience climbing the mountain with heavy buckets, and how I froze as I was overwhelmed by my fear of heights.

Well, I moved forward by keeping it simple. One step at a time. Right and left.

In a complicated world, we must make the same progress.

As we move forward, we must learn to *combine multiple forces* to create *maximum output*.

For example, we all have different backgrounds. That makes each of us unique. We balance our background with our desired destination – our hoped-for future.

Our background provides *push*, and, at the same time, we *pull* ourselves toward our goals. Feel how it works?

No matter how busy and chaotic my life gets, I think of the Katana as a reminder of balance to cut through the complexity and defeat the small enemies. Push. Pull. Right. Left.

In life, balance gives us the stability to create maximum output.

Again, this is simple, yet difficult.

There are many times I feel overwhelmed – pulled in one direction or another.

I'm sure you often experience this same frustration.

During these times, our life feels out of balance. What's more, we're not sure if we're going in the right direction.

But, if we can once more find a balance point, things usually resolve themselves.

Keep your balance – and know that sometimes you will struggle to achieve and maintain that balance in your everyday life.

And that's the point. It's a changing world.

Finding the right balance will always challenge you. Feel it. Realize that the balance point is always moving. In an ever-changing world, balance is a process.

the yellow River
ACHIEVING BALANCE

Balance isn't something you pick up at the store.

Maintaining balance in your life is difficult. And, as we noted, it is always changing.

So even if you are lucky enough to find a moment of balance in your life, a changing world will unexpectedly throw you off balance again.

Achieving balance is a constant process.

You will have to try different combinations until you find the correct one for you.

The Yin and Yang teaches us that balance is the management of coexisting interests.

The Katana teaches us that a balance of forces creates maximum output in our lives.

Time for another story…

The Shaolin Temple was not the only place where I trained. I also spent some time at a small martial arts school on Beijing's far west side.

The teachers there showed me quite a few interesting things.

They took me on many short field trips. I saw the spectacular Great Wall of China – an astonishing feat of engineering and human ingenuity.

It rolls over rugged terrain and splits the forest like a concrete river.

They took me to The Forbidden City – a luxurious fortress that once housed the Emperor of China.

There were many amazing places I was able to visit, but the most influential field trip came from a visit to an unlikely location.

My coach took me to a small fishing town on the banks of the Yellow River – one of the largest rivers in the world and referred to as "the cradle of Chinese civilization."

Today, it is a highly industrialized area, which has caused serious environmental problems.

However, there are still small towns in the region that rely on fishing for a livelihood.

We sat beside the river and watched the fishermen hustle and bustle in their rustic wooden boats. Some would roll up their pant legs and walk out into the river.

They would cast out nets in pairs and reel them in hoping for a big catch. It was the Eastern version of life on the Mississippi.

It was quite peaceful watching this small fishing town operate.

A fisherman came up to us, and we talked about fishing. He told me that the fishermen were working extra hard at present, because it was the best time to fish.

I was a little confused. I asked, why was fishing so important at this time? He gave a surprised look, and responded, "The full moon is coming." Then he walked away.

Well, it turns out that during the full moon, the tides are at their highest and lowest points. These tides influence the activity of the fish, and this makes it the best time to fish.

I saw a new level of balance.

These fishermen achieved balance by *working in harmony with their environment.*

Now, your life may not require you to fish for a living, but we all must learn to work in harmony with the elements around us.

Try to understand all the other forces at work – the coexisting interests and moving parts involved. Just as a fisherman must know the river and the forces that influence it, you too must know the forces in your environment.

Is it a classroom? An office? A household? You already know the environment, but are you really thinking about the rhythm of the forces at work?

Just as the fisherman waits for the full moon for the best fishing, balance your strengths to be in harmony with your environment.

Finding that right combination of coexisting forces and the level of energy to give each can be the most difficult part of finding balance.

But once you begin to think this way you may be surprised at how productive it can be.

Think about balance. Feel it.

Use your judgment to find the correct balance for you. As you start to think this way, I bet you find your judgment will improve.

Remember the lesson of Yin and Yang – it's

not all one way or the other.

Remember the lesson of the Katana – opposing forces can combine. Push/pull. Step by step.

Yes, Kung Fu is hard work, but the game of life is won by those who keep their balance.

Just as the fisherman understands the best fishing conditions are created by the tides, you, too, must know yourself and your environment.

Once you understand the conditions needed for your success, you will be more prepared for opportunity. When you are in balance you will be better able to take advantage of those opportunities as they arise.

Fishermen go to work every day. But they know the best time to go after the big catch.

You will not achieve balance overnight. And, since forces are always changing, finding balance will always be a process. Step by step.

Keep at it. More and more, you will find yourself working from your optimal balance point.

Steps You Can Take

The Dragon is strong, but *balanced*. Yin and Yang teaches us that life is not so black and white.

Balance occurs when you get the multiple interests to coexist.

The Katana teaches us that it is important to make the most of a balance of forces for maximum output.

On the banks of the Yellow River we learned that we achieve balance by working in harmony with our environment.

This may seem like a lot to digest, but let's try to take a step or two. Achieving balance is a process.

Here is a start. *Prioritize*. Ask yourself what is important to you. The goal of the fisherman is to catch fish. Nice and simple. How about you?

Once you've decided on a few priorities, you should institute a system of *Time Management* to balance your time and energy with what is truly important.

Time is always working against you, and we know the world is full of many small enemies.

In life, you are going to have to manage family, career, education, finances, friends, and more. Prioritize.

Make a list of what is most important to you. Like the checklist you made earlier, this list will act as a reminder of your priorities.

Prioritize them and balance the time and attention you give each one based on its level of priority.

Are you going to try out for the TV watching team? If not, maybe that should get less attention. Video games are fun (hey, I'm *in* some of them), but how much of your valuable time do they deserve? Once you start to think about balance, you may be surprised. Take control of your time. It's your time. Prioritize.

Think about the things you'd like to get done.

More likely than not, other things can wait.

Do not put off things that are important to you.

The choice is yours, and this choice will define the balance that is right for you.

Over time, you may find that managing by prioritizing can work in many facets of your life.

Learn to keep your balance when the things around you (whether they be physical or emotional) are out of balance.

Look at the resources in your environment. Are you fishing where the fish are? Are you doing it at the right time? You may need to make changes to achieve a better balance.

If there is a key resource missing or if the environment is not working for your goals, then go out and find a better environment or acquire that missing resource. Find what you need to put your life in balance. Be patient, things will not just happen overnight.

Timing can also be important. Sometimes you must grind your way, but when the opportunity presents itself, attack that opportunity.

When *your* full moon comes, own it.

Find that better balance point.

Maintain your balance. Review your priorities and be sure to give yourself the time to work on what's important to you.

It's your time.

Try to take at least an hour out of your day for selfish reasons to work towards accomplishing one of your goals.

It may be a slow process. There may be trial and error. But if you have the tenacity to keep at it, you will find more balance as you take your journey through life. Step by step.

Kung Fu. Health. Balance.

We're getting good.

Now we need to get better.

It is time to turn our attention to developing Skills.

Skills

tools to Climb A Mountain

We need skills to climb our mountains.

That's the next step in building our Kung Fu Consciousness – working on developing skills.

What do we want to be when we grow up?

We are often asked this question.

On what skills should we focus?

Achieving the answer to this question will define each of us in many ways.

If you want to become a blacksmith, you have to develop the skills necessary to be a blacksmith.

Then, you will "become" the skill.

The trick is finding a skill that fits both your desires in life and the opportunities that exist in your environment. (Not much need for a black-smith these days.)

When you choose a skill, you are beginning to choose a path.

As you develop a skill, you are growing as an individual.

At the Shaolin Temple we were always working on a variety of skills.

One skill I developed was Chinese calligraphy – the art of painting Chinese characters on a large canvas with a special brush and ink.

The practice dates back centuries, and is an important part of the Chinese culture. Each person's calligraphy is unique to that individual.

It's like a signature, only a deeper reflection of the individual.

My instructor went so far as to tell me that calligraphy is a critical practice in combat. Legend says that you could learn a man's sword technique by studying his calligraphy, because both require the same stroke of the wrist.

That may be an exaggerated interpretation of

legend, but there is one important thing I learned from developing skill in calligraphy – individualism.

Your individualism is a key element in the value you provide to society. In life, as in calligraphy, no two people are exactly the same.

The stroke of a brush reflects each of us.

How will your skills reflect on you as an individual? It's an important consideration.

There are two broad categories of skills everyone should have – hard skills and soft skills.

My Calligraphy Class in The Shaolin Temple

Choose Your Weapon
HARD SKILLS

At the Shaolin Temple, every Monk will have a specific category to master.

Meditation Monks focus on the practice of meditation. Martial Monks only practice martial arts.

There are even Medicine Monks. Right – they only practice medicine.

In some ways, it's similar to a Western university setting. All Monks go through a general education system. Each is given the opportunity to learn the basics of different fields.

Then, they specialize.

The Martial Monks generally choose one weapon and one form of hand-to-hand combat.

They might have a good overall understanding of several different forms of martial arts, but they eventually focus on just one skill.

They become really good at one weapon.

If they split their attention between multiple weapons they might be very "good" at several things, but not "great" at any of them.

For each of us, choosing a skill is much like choosing a weapon. We can't be good at everything.

At some point you must "choose your weapon." You will need to decide what you want to specialize in. Later, you can expand or branch out, but, in the beginning, you need to ask yourself what skill you want to offer.

The Hook Swords

Every skill has its value. When I first began my training I was only interested in the fighting aspects of the Shaolin Temple.

I guess you could say I had tunnel vision.

I never really paid attention to the other arts. I was kind of a jerk about it. I looked at the other categories as weaker, because they did not require the strength required for fighting.

This ignorance limited my development. I was not open to learning new things. So it was time for some difficult lessons.

During that time, a close family member and mentor of mine was diagnosed with cancer.

Cancer is a vicious enemy. Watching my friend lose that battle was devastating for me.

At this point, I began to understand the value of categories and skills other than fighting.

I understood the lessons the Monks tried to teach me – that fighting is just a small part of the skills we need for life.

In our modern society, the ability to fight is not very valuable outside of sports and self-defense.

Who cares if you know how to fight? The sharpest sword cannot defeat cancer. The hardest punch will not help you succeed at work.

There is more to life than combat.

To win other battles, we need other skills.

What skill will you choose?

For a start, try to pick something you enjoy doing. This is good advice. Because more likely than not it is a skill you will be using for the rest of your life.

Give some thought to deciding what you want to do. How do you decide? Look to the needs of society. Is it a skill that is needed?

Try to find a skill that has some foreseeable demand. The more society needs your skill, the more value you will add to society.

Once you have chosen your hard skills, you will need to balance those skills with soft skills.

Stroke the Horse's Mane
SOFT SKILLS

To succeed in life we need to complement our hard, technical skills with soft, "people" skills.

With calligraphy, I discovered you cannot succeed with brute force. Instead, you must allow your wrist to gently guide your brush.

My teacher instructed me to paint as though I was brushing a horse's mane. If you use too much pressure the horse will kick you, but if you stroke it just right, the horse will be calm.

When it came to calligraphy, I was a clumsy student. It seemed I could never get the characters to come out right. I often found myself the butt of jokes during class.

I had difficulty holding the brush correctly.

I would get ink everywhere.

Sometimes the teacher would ask us to show our best work in front of the entire class. Other students would giggle when I approached the front of the class. My work was that bad.

I practiced over and over again, but I never saw any significant improvement. I became irritated and confused at the same time.

I could not understand it. I always thought I could just put my head down and grind through any situation. Sometimes you have to take a step back.

My Calligraphy Class in The Shaolin Temple

That's what I had to do. I began to visualize my characters and break them down into strokes and energy, which is what calligraphy requires.

Similarly in life, there are many instances where the gentle stroke of the brush can overcome the blunt strike of the sword.

We need to understand that soft, "people" skills can be just as important as those hard skills.

As you acquire skills, you must also turn your attention to the "art" of applying them to society.

After all, if you cannot use your skills to work with people in society, your skills do not really have much value.

Take a step back. Try to understand the reasons people might need your skills. Put yourself in the shoes of others.

Whether hard or soft, acquiring each skill demands Kung Fu – hard work. Your skill is something you use for others.

Hard or soft, they both demand your best.

Now that you understand the two categories, let's turn our attention to developing them.

Student + Master
THE SIFU

Teachers help us acquire skills.

At the Shaolin Temple, students refer to their instructor as "Sifu" (SHEE-FU).

The Monks taught me the term means "father figure." There were many reasons to look upon your instructor as a father figure.

The Sifu not only teaches a specific subject, but is also a mentor in life. This creates a close relationship between student and teacher.

Each has a vested interest in the other.

The first stage of your development is to be a student. The journey of a student can be very special. Respect it. Try to enjoy it.

When you are a student, respect your teachers. They are your guides to success in life.

When my training began at The Shaolin Temple, all I did was listen. If I spoke out of turn, I was harshly disciplined.

As a student, the "action" is to listen and understand. The point of speaking is to ask questions.

The student phase of your development can be difficult. There is no easy way to skip this process. It is time consuming, humbling, and often painful. Being a student is also Kung Fu. It is hard work.

However, we receive a reward. We grow and become better at our skills.

Others around you are building their skills.

Competition is often part of the skill-building process. We learn a lot from competition.

First, it shows you where you stand. Second, it can motivate you to work harder.

As you develop as a student, you slowly start to become a Sifu yourself.

One of the best ways to further polish your skills is to teach them. Those who do not give back are like guns that shoot only blanks. They might look impressive and make great noise, but they have no real impact.

Developing others is very important to your growth. We learn. We teach.

Steps You Can Take

In addition to discipline, we have choice.

What *Hard Skills* and *Soft Skills* will we choose to climb our mountain?

As you develop your skills, you will start as a student, but end as a teacher. This is the journey.

Now what are we going to do about it?

There are many different ways to choose and develop a skill.

The process I like best is finding a *mentor*. You seek out and then interact with established people in their fields.

You look for some sort of apprenticeship. It may be as deep as becoming an intern. Or you may only read about the person. Or perhaps get his or her recommendations for improvement (such as books to read or instructional videos).

We don't need to become Jamie Oliver's friend to improve our cooking skills.

This process teaches many different values. First, it can help you choose your skill. With expert help, you will find out firsthand whether the skill is something you want to do for the rest of your life.

Second, mentoring develops "people skills."

It teaches humility and respect. The process is humbling, because you are asking for help.

Choose a skill and find mentors. They may be people you meet – or it may be their help comes from books or videos or courses in school.

Become a Sifu!

As we said, one of the best ways to learn is to teach – once you find some direction.

You should select a hard skill – one that will make you more valuable and you should also work on your soft skills – those that make you a better friend and family member.

A simple way to think about incorporating any skill into your life is to create a balance of science and art. The science is your "Hard Skill." The art is your "Soft Skill."

The first step is simple, but complex – like so many things. You must decide which skill you would like to develop. Every job in the world requires certain skill sets, and every skill has both hard and soft characteristics.

Ask yourself what you want to be when you grow up. Make it easy on yourself. What makes you happy in life? There is opportunity to make a career in every field.

Not every skill needs to be your career. Cooking, playing a musical instrument, or improving your handwriting (calligraphy) are all skills that can enrich your life.

And, of course, you might consider some skill that has career improvement implications.

If you are miserable in your job, then find one that does not make you miserable. Or try to find a way to restructure your job to make it more tolerable. Since this is about Kung-Fu, you might consider working harder.

Whatever you choose, try to choose your skill strategically.

Just like a good baseball manager will strategically place players in the best possible positions and batting order, you, too, should choose your position based on making the most of your abilities and opportunities for success.

Try to know yourself inside and outside. Be honest about your strengths and your weaknesses.

How will you make the most of your strengths while minimizing your weaknesses? The choice is yours. But make it a choice, not an accident.

For example, if mathematics is one of your weaker subjects, either invest the time to turn it into your strength, or choose a profession that does not heavily rely on math.

Either way, you probably want to learn something like Quicken, so you have the skill to balance your checkbook and keep those credit card bills under control.

Your decision may involve risks.

If you choose something with a low probability of success, then you make your choice with the understanding that it might lead nowhere. It may not be a risk worth taking. Or maybe it is.

Once you make this decision, you will have

to work your butt off to get there. Hard work, remember?

And improving that skill will probably require finding a teacher – either in books or in person – who will help you improve your skills. It will also probably require you to improve your skill at being a student.

One way to test your caliber of *hard skills* and *soft skills* is to try teaching someone else. You really learn a lot from teaching.

A law school professor once told me that he was not in the teaching business, but, rather, in the entertainment industry. He needed to know the substance of the skill he was teaching, but he also needed to be entertaining enough to engage his students and have them pay attention to him.

You know what I am talking about. Have you ever sat in a lecture or class where the speaker is boring or monotonous? It is torture. It is difficult to stay awake, let alone learn anything.

This is an example of weak soft skills. Sad to say, it doesn't matter what the teacher knows, if he or she is not conveying the scientific substance of the material in a way that helps people connect with the material.

Teach. Learn. Teach. Learn.

Balance the science of your *hard skills* with the art of your *soft skills*. This is a great way to exercise, and it's a great way to improve your skill level.

Enjoy it, for you will be doing it for the rest of your life.

Goals

目標

the top of the mountain

You must have goals. You must choose which mountain to climb.

This is the final step – choosing a mountain to climb.

When I first arrived at the Shaolin Temple, my goal was to learn at the birthplace of martial arts.

I'd already spent a great deal of time in my life learning martial arts. Training at the Temple symbolized "coming full circle" for me.

My path was somewhat unconventional…

When I was a teenager, I was the target of bullies. I was small and had no one to defend me.

Although bullies terrorized me for years, my breaking point came when I was in my early teens.

I remember the experience very clearly. Five members of a local gang cornered me in the back of a bus and beat me up.

As I was being pummeled, I remember my body frozen with fear. I did not even try to fight back. The bullies stopped after a few minutes. Maybe they were bored.

As I lay bloody on the floor of the bus, I hit my breaking point.

It was time to stand up for myself. I felt that I had nothing left to lose.

I began to take my martial arts training very seriously. I did not expect to become a superhero. I simply decided that if they would continue to attack me, I would not go down without a fight.

It did not happen overnight. The bullying continued for a while. But something was different. As my body and mind slowly became stronger, the bullies slowly stopped bothering me. Somehow they just knew.

It was then that I discovered that bullies are actually cowards. They prey on the weak.

At the Shaolin Temple, the bravest fighters want to defend the weak and fight the strong. It is when you stand up to fight the best, that you see where you stand in life.

Bullies hide behind their size and numbers.

Heroes step forward despite the odds.

Training at the Shaolin Temple represented the top of the mountain. A wise man once told me I should thank those bullies. It is because of them that I set this goal and began this amazing journey.

The ceremony of entry into the Temple was quite grand. We stood in two single file lines outside the front doors of the Temple.

I felt like the closed gates represented a secret society. The Temple's doors are closed off to the rest of the world. Inside were the answers to many of my questions.

Somehow, I believed the Shaolin Temple would provide me with the answer to the meaning of life.

Sounds crazy, right? It gets crazier.

As we stood in line, the huge wooden gates of the Temple began to open as a pounding drum provided a rhythmic backdrop.

One of the head Monks came out in a bright orange robe. All the students dropped to one knee.

The Monk instructed us to take an oath. You swear to follow the rules of the Temple.

The Monk then left. We were instructed not to move until he returned. It was about four hours.

After that long wait, remaining virtually motionless, I remember hearing the heavy doors open. I breathed a sigh of relief at the simple pleasure of just being able to move. I entered the Temple and began my journey.

In retrospect, the Shaolin Temple did teach me the meaning of life.

Time for another story.

As I was kneeling in front of the Temple waiting to be admitted, the thought of training with some of the best martial artists in the world almost overwhelmed me.

What if I did not have what it takes?

What if I had come all this way only to fail?

I felt like they could smell my fear.

I was more than a little intimidated at the challenge before me.

But, despite my fears, I never turned back. Why? Because I had a *goal*.

That goal gave me a *purpose*. That purpose was stronger than my fears.

Purpose gives life meaning

Purpose helped me overcome my fears.

Purpose drove me to the top of my mountain.

Your purpose can change. Your goal can change, but the power of having a goal endures in our hearts and keeps us moving forward.

Goals are an important part of our lives. They provide direction and destination. When you have a destination, you are walking with purpose.

You know where you are going and why.

So think about it.

What is your purpose? Are you adding to the overall benefit of society? Are you improving your ability to add to that benefit?

Do not dismiss small goals. These too, help shape our lives. Winning gold medals is good – so is preparing a healthy breakfast. Every day is full of small goals. Being on time. Getting things done. Improving grades from a "C" to a "B."

All too often, people live without a sense of purpose. This is like food without flavor.

Do not deny yourself the privilege of purpose. Like a meal, even a small goal can be delicious and enough for the moment. Once you discover a larger purpose, a mountain to climb, the adventure of life will stretch before you.

Cursed are those who live without purpose, for they never truly discover who they are.

And now I think you know that even if you do not yet have a larger goal, you will be happier when you have one.

Happiness. Another step worth taking.

The Chinese Zodiac
HAPPINESS:

One main goal in life should be happiness.

Again, simple but complicated. Everyone has a different definition of happiness.

The Shaolin Monks had a tool to categorize people – the Chinese Zodiac.

The Chinese Zodiac has a twelve-year cycle. Each year is represented by an animal.

Under the Chinese Zodiac, the year you are born will match up to a particular animal. It is suggested that you will have the same characteristics and traits of that animal.

Oversimplified, it says the year you were born tells us the type of person you are. But we know that everyone our own age in school was not the same.

For example, I was born in the Year of the Ram. It is common belief in the Chinese culture that the Ram carries such characteristics as intelligence and a peaceful nature. Fair enough.

In many ways, I do see these characteristics in myself. Let's see… I enjoy reading and learning about history, and I love solving problems. I enjoy the challenge. But, there are definitely times I branch out from the standard definition.

For example, an interest in martial arts does not seem to indicate a peaceful nature. Or does it? The Shaolin Monks taught me that I must fight for peace. Hmmm…

Well, let's face it, these characteristics will not be exactly on point for everyone, but I bet each of us can see a few characteristics in our sign.

The Chinese Zodiac does something simple, but complicated. It shows us we are all different and we are all the same.

Training with The Shaolin Monks in the Mountains at Shaolin Temple

As we strive toward our goals, we begin to have a better understanding of what makes us happy.

Unhappy times can remind us of what is truly important. Have you ever suddenly lost a friend or family member? Blam! It puts the world into a new perspective. Suddenly, you do not waste your time thinking about the petty issues that seem to consume a day. It puts things into clear focus.

So does one other thing – the Declaration of Independence.

It states that we are all entitled to "the pursuit of happiness." I'm sure the Shaolin Monks would agree.

When we have goals, we are, in a very real way, *pursuing* happiness.

For each of us, it is different, but the same – just like the Chinese Zodiac.

Maintaining Your Purpose

As the things that can fill our day pile up, it is easy to lose sight of some of our goals.

As we make our way through life, whether we are going top speed or just fighting our way through traffic, we should remember to take some time to enjoy the journey. It is easy to fall victim and fall into the rat race of life.

And remember, it is not just reaching the goal – it is the journey. Enjoy the climb.

There is joy in the journey. Even though some of the steps may be difficult, trust me, they make the taste of even small accomplishments sweeter. Goals and purpose help shape that enjoyment.

A good friend worked at an ad agency whose logo was a hand reaching for the stars. The words that accompanied that visual recognized the world that we live in – "When you reach for the stars, you may not get one, but you won't come up with a handful of mud either."

At the end of the day, be happy. Our time here is limited. That's reason enough to savor every day.

Water
ADAPTATION:

The world around us changes. So do we.

One way to stay happy is by being adaptive.

Our final topic will be adaptability.

Things will not always go your way.

Learn to adjust. Set a new goal.

Make yourself adaptable to any circumstance.

Think in terms of water.

This is a difference between East and West. In Western society, our stories are of conquering obstacles and winning through. Well and good.

In the more crowded worlds of the East, they know that not every obstacle can be conquered – and if we cannot change the world around us, that means we must change ourselves.

This is not defeat.

This is life.

We change and make the most of our circumstances – like water.

Water is one of the most adaptable substances on Earth. Water can take any shape or form when needed. Water can generate powerful pounding waves, and the very same water can create a calm, peaceful pond.

Other forces can influence water. If it is cold the water will freeze. If it is hot the water will boil and evaporate. However, regardless of circumstance, it never stops being water.

Water is the most abundant element in the human body. So, in many ways you can say that water and humans are very much in harmony.

We have that same power of adaptability.

Take a lesson from water. Adapt your goals — no matter the circumstance.

There is a lesson here. We must embrace and anticipate change. For example, think in terms of your job. It will always be your responsibility as a professional to adapt yourself to changing times. And times will always change.

As times change, your job may not add value as it did before. Think about a manufacturer of the cassette tape. Remember cassettes? Not too many job openings for that position right now.

If you are still in school, embrace that change and the sequence of goals you set for yourself.

See if you can take an extra class or seminar to become a better student or professional. Attend conferences or join groups so you can see how others do their jobs. Anticipate changes in your industry.

Things you do for extra credit are not done for the teacher – they are done for you. One more goal to enjoy. More happiness to pursue.

Will we catch what we pursue? Every once in a while. Enjoy the chase.

I realize that all this is easier said than done, but who said life was easy? Sometimes loving parents try to make it easier. Appreciate their love, but realize that goals are the result of effort – they are not handed to us. Nor should they be.

As I think of my life, I think of the journey I am on. I have just shared a part of that journey with you.

We each walk a path trying to get to our destination. Sometimes the path is already made. Sometimes we have to build a new one. Sometimes the goal – the destination – changes. We learn on our journey.

Sometimes we become so focused on the goal that we do not enjoy the journey, learn the lessons, or appreciate what we see along the route.

Even with goals firmly in mind, we never really know where life will take us. The lessons I learned at the Shaolin Temple were not what I expected. Still, having the goal of studying there helped me keep moving forward. Step by step.

Your journey and the route you take and the sights you see will be the basis for your experience.

Some prefer to drive slowly through life and enjoy the view. Others will drive hard – pedal to the metal.

The cool thing is this – the path you take and the speed you travel are your choice. Choosing your goals, making your own path, and going at your own speed are part of the joy of the journey of life.

We each have the power to choose the way we live our lives, set our goals, and pursue our happiness.

And one thing that helps us know where we are going is having goals. They may change. You may have to adapt. But our life works better when we have them.

Training for the game of life

Steps You Can Take

Bullies are cowards. They prey on the weak. Heroes stand and fight – no matter the odds.

We also learned that the journey of life goes better when you have purpose – *goals*.

The *Chinese Zodiac* reminds us that we are different, but the same. We also learned that in a changing world, we must learn to adapt. We must be like *water*.

When I was a teenager, my goals were simple: to survive my bus ride home from school.

That simple goal gave my life a purpose. Your purpose defines you and drives you to discover yourself. My goal eventually drove me to the Shaolin Temple.

Where will your goals lead you?

Each of us will have our own unique way of discovering our purpose in life.

We will each begin to create goals.

Many struggle to find those things that make them happy and to define their goals – so they postpone the decision. Odd as this sounds, one approach I would suggest is to take a deep breath and take a step back.

Taking time away from everything will make you appreciate those things that are truly important to you. Maybe try a bit of meditation.

Another story.

One day, while meditating in the mountains, I had a sudden rush of emotion.

I experienced a revelation.

Training at the Temple had pushed me to my very limits. At this point, I realized what was truly important to me.

Happiness for me was taking care of loved ones. I had been away from them and I missed them dearly.

It was so simple, I felt kind of stupid.

I thought, "Why did I put myself through all this just to discover what was right in front of me?"

As it turns out, one key to my happiness was not at the top of some tall mountain, but simply within the comforts of my own home.

I experienced complete Zen with this answer. One main purpose in my life was to care for my friends and family. Any other goal or accomplishment would be meaningless if I failed at this one.

Work hard. Be tenacious. Respect our health. Develop our skills. And set goals.

Each of these is a step on the path to the "Victorious Life."

the Edge of the Cliff
CONCLUSION

Thank you for taking this journey with me.

I learned a lot about life living as a Monk in the Shaolin Temple. Now I've had the time to absorb the principles taught there.

With this book I wanted to share that journey and some of the lessons I learned in the hope they might be useful for your own journey.

I hope that the process of achieving Kung Fu Consciousness helped you begin the search to "Discover Your Dragon."

Like a Dragon, we must learn balance. Science and art. Head and heart. Soft skills and hard.

This book is no "all-inclusive" answer.

It simply attempts to show you how some ancient Eastern principles apply to your modern life. Because many of today's problems are actually timeless – and so are the steps we can take to solve them.

We began this book with a story.

I would now like to finish that story.

You will remember how I talked about climbing a mountain carrying heavy buckets of water.

That day, I did not enjoy the journey.

I learned that I had made that dangerous trek up the mountain simply to water a tree.

After I watered the tree I was able to set down the buckets and let my arms rest. I enjoyed the welcome relief on my shoulders. I momentarily dropped to the ground to catch my breath. It was a deep breath without strain.

I was still far from the edge of the cliff, as the dizzying height made me uncomfortable.

Among the Cliffs of Shaolin Temple

I still had troubling thoughts.

I was embarrassed from the breakdown that had come from my fear of heights combined with my exhaustion as I climbed the stairs.

Slightly recovered, I walked over to the Monk who had helped calm me down.

I wanted to thank him.

He smiled and walked me toward the cliff.

I followed apprehensively, though I did not get too close to the edge.

As I slowly became more comfortable, I took in a deep breath of the cold fresh mountain air.

Then, I took in the inspiring view.

No description would do it justice.

The memory will be engraved in my mind for the rest of my life.

I stepped closer to the edge to get a better look at the magnificent view. I forgot my fear of heights. I even had the courage to look down.

The Monk looked at me, smiled slightly, and asked, "Was the journey worth it?"

I took a moment to reflect.

I had to conquer my fear of heights as I carried two heavy buckets of water up a dangerous mountain trail in the freezing cold – all to water a tree.

I replied, "This is a beautiful view, but I had to endure significant struggles to get here."

The Monk answered, "That is the way of life."

*Amituofo**

---

*   *Amatuofo* is a traditional salutation among Shaolin Monks. It literally translates to "Buddha of Infinite Light."

About the Author

KungFu-Cious is Donald Hyun Kiolbassa. He is a gold medalist for the United States Chinese Martial Arts Team (Traditional World Games, 2008 China). He studied martial arts while living in seclusion at the Shaolin Temple with the Shaolin Monks (by invitation) and Wudan Mountain in China. His martial arts abilities have lead him to do entertainment work for Disney and Warner Brothers. He is the man behind the moves of several monumental video games. He has studied extensively throughout Asia and Latin America. He is a licensed attorney and licensed Certified Public Accountant (KPMG LLP alumni). During his free time, he is an adjunct law professor and serves on the boards of several charitable organizations.

Special Acknowledgements

I would like to thank all of the readers of this book for taking time to share their thoughts. I would like to thank The Shaolin Temple for inviting me to live and train there with the Monks in seclusion.

I would like to thank Dominic Cianciolo for teaching me the art of storytelling.

I would also like to thank my life mentors Joseph Bachewicz, Franco LaMarca, Mark Pedowitz, Craig Hunegs, Larry Kaufman, Rabbi Colman Ginsparg, Dick Bolton, Professor Rory Smith, Chef Dave Choi, and Dr. Michael Fang. Thank you all for giving me direction!

I would like to thank my Kung Fu brothers and friends Pakorn Pongpaet, Sifu Tim Wright, Jeffery Nobleza, Ralph McConnell, Sifu Philip Sahagun, Wesley Scarpias Gonzales, Dr. Nick Leroy, Jonny Oh, Gene Ching, Gigi Oh (the whole Tigerclaw family), Sensei Michael Bach, and James Bach (The whole HERO Fitness family). I am honored to call each of you my friend.

I would like to thank my most influential martial arts instructors Tian HaiHong, Sifu Anthony Marquez, Sifu Daniel Pesina, and Sifu Carlos Pesina. I am honored to call each of you "teacher," and there is no way to repay the debt I owe to each of you.

Finally, I would like to thank my publishers Bruce and Lorelei Bendinger. I love you both!